# My Verses

## An Anthology of Poems & Songs Based Upon One Man's Trials & Tribulations

### Adrian Young

GW00400059

My Verses

Copyright © 2022 by Adrian Young

First Edition - Published in 2022.

ISBN 9798366948258 (Paperback)

For Amelie

*Hard, long times*
*A cease of thoughts in endless rhymes*
*Who am I*
*To write the words you choose to like?*

# About the Author

Adrian Young was born on the east coast of England, within the seaside town of Great Yarmouth, in 1985, and was the second son of Julie and the first child to Alan. He has one older brother, Marcus, and a young daughter, Amelie.

Attending Herman first and middle schools, in Gorleston-on-Sea, Adrian soon developed a love of books from a young age, often enjoying Allan Ahlberg's collection of *Funnybones* stories, as well as the works of the wonderful Roald Dahl and Enid Blyton. He also quickly became an avid reader of true crime, which grew from his dad's collection of books within that genre and aided in developing his love for true crime documentaries.

As he grew into his teens, whilst attending Oriel High School, Adrian began writing short stories and poems, with much of his inspiration stemming from his love of 50s and 60s music, which was introduced to him by his step-father, Robert, who also taught Adrian how to play the guitar.

One of Adrian's earliest stories was born from his love of the legendary Johnny Cash song, 'Folsom Prison Blues', where Adrian reimagined Cash's lyrics to create a short story of a man struggling to come to terms with life within the prison system. This particular story was submitted as coursework, for which Adrian received much praise from his English teacher. This event acted as a catalyst for Adrian to take a more in-depth interest in writing.

After leaving high school in 2001, Adrian went straight into full-time work, whilst performing weekly in a rock and roll band, The Open Shells.

Music increased Adrian's creativity rapidly from the age of 18, when he began to compose his own songs.

Inspired by the autobiographical nature of artists such as John Lennon, as well as the wordplay of Bob Dylan, Adrian's collection of songs rapidly grew.

As Adrian acquainted himself with the highs and lows of life, he drew on his experiences and continued to put pen to paper, which, to date, has led to him writing over one hundred compositions.

As Adrian's confidence grew, he began to perform more frequently, both as a solo artist and as part of various bands, duos, and trios. In 2017, along with his colleague, Nicholas Kitson, Adrian entered a local talent contest. Never expecting to win, Adrian and Nick were shocked when it was announced they had came in first place, with comments from the judges stating it was Adrian's originality and song-writing abilities which won them over.

In 2018, Adrian became a father to Amelie Isla Young, and it was his daughter who reignited Adrian's desire to write again.

As the joys and strains of parenthood flowed through Adrian's life, he daydreamed of writing more songs, more poems, and more stories. He began reading more, enhancing his knowledge of the English language, and looking at life from a different perspective.

Adrian still lives in Norfolk, England, where he fulfils his passion for writing, hoping to bring happiness to others and to make his daughter proud.

# Introduction

The first time I ever sat and dedicated time to writing a song was when I was about eighteen years old. I had just joined my first band, The Open Shells, and the lead vocalist, Graham Stacey, had written several songs which we would perform regularly around the local pubs and clubs.

The band coincided with a burst of passion I developed for music. I had been listening studiously to The Beatles, Bob Dylan, Buddy Holly, and many other artists who helped define their generation. I surrounded myself with music from the 1950s, through to the modern day, and although I had yet to find my own way of working; I knew I had to ability to write songs.

My first writing session is something I recall vividly. I was sitting in my bedroom at my dad's house, acoustic guitar in one hand, pen in the other, a large notebook in front of me, with *Bob Dylan's Greatest Hits* playing in the background. I strummed my guitar, alternating chords, hoping for inspiration to strike.

I played a basic blues rhythm in the key of A on my Crafter guitar, repeating it relentlessly until words and melodies crept through. Two hours later, I had written my first song, 'Come and Go'. I presented it to the band at our next rehearsal. It worked well, and the band received the composition positively. Sadly, I had yet to find my singing voice, and as good as the song sounded, my singing was off key, with no emotion shining through.

Almost twenty years later, I have written many more songs and poems, using the medium as a form of emotional release. Whether I feel happiness, love, fear, sadness, depression, anxiety, or any other feeling, writing forms part of my life, and I cannot envisage that ever changing.

Contained within these pages are reflections of my life at the time of which they were written. Most are accompanied by the story of how those words came about, whilst others, I felt, were best left to your own imagination.

I sincerely hope that you enjoy the words contained within this book. They may even connect with your own personal experiences, thoughts, and emotions. That is the beauty of art; you can connect to it in the most unexpected ways.

Thank you for taking the time to read my book. If you enjoy its content, you will find further information on my works, as well as various ways in which you can follow my publications and contact me, at the end of this book.

# Contents

# Come and Go

It seems fitting that the first song I ever wrote sits as the first in this book. The lyrics are that of an eighteen-year-old man, trying to figure out how to be a bit like Bob Dylan, or perhaps somewhat like John Lennon or Paul McCartney. *How hard can it be?*

As do many youngsters in their late teens, I already felt like I knew how the world worked. I felt like I had experienced enough to know how to circumnavigate *anything* which life may throw at me. Regardless of such naivety, I soon learnt that I could not possibly know *everything*.

I was listening to the Beatles' *Revolver* album relentlessly around the time 'Come and Go' was composed, which inspired the use of the word 'revolving' within its third verse. I also lifted the title of John Lennon's 'Borrowed Time' within the same fragment.

The lyrics reflect an attempt at being deep and meaningful, but the naivety of youth shines through.

1

Well, I'm thinking that I've seen it all
But I'm not getting any wiser
And, this life, you know, it can be short
So, the people are a little divided

I've seen them come, but they always go
They have the attitude for the rock 'n' roll
A little wiser - just a bit too slow
You must forget the past, so now you let it go

Everybody's lives are revolving
And we're all stuck in borrowed time
And your faith, you know, is often controlling
But every day of my life is fine

And we're all that little bit different
Yes, we all have to let go at times
And we never know what we're concealing
Just as long as we speak our minds

I've seen them come, but they always go
They have the attitude for the rock 'n' roll
A little wiser - just a bit too slow
You must forget the past, so now you let it go

# I Am One

It has always been important to me to write from the heart. In my mind, honest art is the *best* art.

'I Am One' is a poem which I hold dear to me, as it is one of my most honest moments I have had in my writing, as I faced up to some demons I had at that stage in my life.

The 'green-eyed monster' is something that is in all of us. We all get jealous, but what is important is how we manage that jealousy and what we learn from it.

Written in 2006, just after my 21st birthday, I realised that jealousy was causing difficulties for me and I wanted to reflect on it, and learn from my mistakes. Pen in hand, I wrote how I felt. This process developed into 'I Am One' and is written in a conversational style whereby I am communicating with the emotion, letting it know how I feel, hoping to come to a resolution.

I've been waiting around here
For, God Knows, way too long
Don't you try to argue now
Because I'll always prove you wrong

Every time I run and hide
You'll track me down along the line
I can't seem to get away
From my evil, jealous mind

Something hides, it's deep inside
A crawling stage on a Sunday night
Like a pain, won't go away
You're on my mind and here to stay

As my spirit learns to crawl
Knock my head against a wall
Looks like I can't run away
A state of mind that's here to stay

Pacing up and down a room
Hoping this will all end soon
Living life like it's a game
Nothing's real, it's all the same

So, if I turn and run away
Will you chase me down again?

My mind is old, but I am young
I feel nothing. I am one
I feel nothing. I am one

# The Music Man

Clear across the border of all we know
He revels in the pain
Singing words for the soul
He taps his feet down upon the floor
As he looks into your eyes
Like a beggar, he is scorned
He doesn't wait a minute just to say how he feels
If he knows he can hurt you
Then he knows you are real
If he can get what he wants
He shall strike where you stand
Because he's just a cruel-hearted music man

He stands in the shadows waiting for the one
The targets cannot hide
For they are under the sun
Moments have passed, then nothing becomes
Something in his eyes
For he is now someone

Who begs and steals, not borrows, if it makes him free
Because the only time he's human
Are the times in which he bleeds
He is not self-conscious
He's his own biggest fan
Because he is just a cruel-hearted music man

So, if you find yourself in his circle of friends
Keep yourself wise as to the games of which he blends
He'll spin you round his words
Until he gets what he needs
For it's upon the pain and sorrow
That you feel where he feeds
So be sure to read his words
Because that's where he shows
What his true emotions are and all that he knows
He won't let no one in, he says
'Friendship is banned'
Because he's just a cruel-hearted music man

# Final Smile

Some of my earliest memories in life involve spending weekends with my dad, Alan James Young, his brother, Frederick Young, and their mum, Alice May Young - known to all as May.

My nanny lived a simplistic life; she enjoyed sitting in her chair, watching the world go by, whilst often reading a book. She cared little for television, other than programs more suited to her generation, such as *The Antiques Roadshow* or *Dad's Army*.

No matter how hard I try, I cannot recall my nanny ever looking younger than my final memories of her. Throughout much of my lifetime, she always had entirely grey hair, which was permed. She was a creature of habit for the styles of clothing she wore and, to the best of my recollection, little changed in her appearance other than the wrinkles, of which we all succumb to.

It came as little surprise to me when my nanny became ill - I was always conscious of her age.

The last time I visited nanny in her care home, as I approached her for the last time, her eyes opened, she looked at me, and she smiled.

Nanny passed away peacefully on April 3, 2007. Nanny May was my first personal experience of loss. Although some of my relatives, such as my grandad, Fred, had passed away, I was too young to know or understand.

*How do I deal with loss?* Like much in my life, the answer came through music. Lyrics began to mean more to me, and I felt like I had a deeper connection with songs after my nanny passed. Lyrics began to make more sense. I discovered how I would address my emotions about nanny's passing – I would write how I felt.

I wanted to ensure the memory of nanny's final smile she gave to me was not forgotten in time, so 'Final Smile' holds particular poignancy in my life.

All that you lost is easily found
Take it in your grasp, go walk away now
Now, I'll take your hand and place it in mine
I was always your friend - I'm so glad you were mine

There was a time when you just seemed lost
Forgot the directions that you've come across
Go 'way from me and find your own way
In this life, it's easy to live day by day

I'm lost in confusion, can't find the time

I need a helping hand and you'll do just fine
You were the first one I lost and I'm sad
It seems I'm confused about what I once had

You left behind all that you loved
I'll never forget you and all that you was
There's one thing for sure
That'll guide me for a while:
I held your hand, and I saw you smile

# Another Day

Another Friday night
Drumming the beats out of my mind
Here, by my side
A lonely guitar with an unstrung heart
Dark glazed eyes
Looking for something to be inspired by

Hard, long times
A cease of thoughts in endless rhymes
Who am I
To write the words you choose to like?
All my life
Carry a weight until the day I die

So long dreams
They passed away through dull-light seams
Can I see
Another way that they're pulling me
Away from heat
To keep me going and give me what I need?

Who am I, in a lost direction?
I can't find my way home
Who am I, to even say
I'll live to learn to fight another day?

# Forward

Written around the same time of my nanny's passing, 'Forward' was created whilst I was withdrawing into myself somewhat. I was of an age where I felt I had little direction in life.

Many of us experience such a period in early adulthood where we suddenly feel like life is running away from us, and we need some kind of stabilisation — a road map of life, so to speak.

The lyrics of 'Forward' vividly display my lack of self-belief, but I feel, despite the glumness of the lyrics, the title symbolises my intention of carrying on and pushing forward.

I'm so tired thinking of the chores
All my pain's just as deep as my soul
I feel you running through my bones

These days don't get easier
Time takes its toll and I'm bleeding, yeah
Won't you come and take it all away?

Standing up, waiting for the sun
It never comes, but I'm staying calm
But you know, I don't believe in me

I don't hold back anything no more
I speak my feelings – I don't hide my thoughts
I'm no longer standing all alone
I've learnt a lot, there's so much more to know

I'm so tired of feeling things I do
I only mess up everything, it's true
I don't believe it all will end

My emotions affect everything
They change my life, and in the way I think
Maybe, someday, in my heart, I will let go

Because I don't hold back what I feel no more
I voice my feelings, whilst never hiding my thoughts
I'm no longer walking all alone
I've learnt a lot, there's always more to know

# She's On My Mind

She says all the things
That I want to hear every day
She does something to me
Which I feel I just cannot explain

When I wake up in the morning
She's the first thing that I see in my mind
What she won't say in words, I just know
Because I can see in her eyes
She's on my mind

She's in a difficult situation
Where she just can't decide
To follow one road or the next
Then just see what she may find

She's stuck right in the middle
And I know she needs to see for herself
That just taking a chance
Is a chance worth taking in itself

She's on my mind

She can feel all the weight
Of the world just hanging around
Like it doesn't matter what she says
Because it's so hard for her, right now

I hope that I make her feel
All the things that I feel
Because I know what I want
And everything that I feel is so real
She's on my mind

# Listen

# (For a Change)

⊹⟫⟩ ⋅ ⋅ ◆ ⋅ ⟨⟨⊹

Throughout my 20s, I became angry with the world. I can't recall at what point exactly, or even the reasons behind such feelings, but I felt frustrated with life, with work, with myself, and with people. I felt as though, despite my continual determination, I was making little progress at achieving the things I hoped to achieve within life. *Why am I not getting recognised for my strengths? Why does no one listen, even when the answer is smacking them in the face repeatedly?*

Feeling we are not being heard is something we all concern ourselves about from time to time, be it with our loved ones, our colleagues, or the stranger in the street. Sometimes, all we want from life is to be listened to.

We sit, we look, we laugh, we cry
We spend our lives just asking why
We see no end in sight, in mind
We seek the truth, but never find a way

We're down, we're out, we're low, not high
We spread our wings, but never fly
We shout and scream to get away
We can't get out, we're here to stay

(and they're)
So wild nights, and we're so wide awake
And if just for once
You could just shut your mouth
And listen for a change!

We cry, we weep, we bow our heads
In shame, for love, to honour the dead
We walk, we run, to stay a while
We fight the dark; we have to smile today

We crawl, we beg, to have the chance
To see that we may finally dance
We hope, we pray, for someday soon
We'll live in peace, not die in ruin

(and they're)

So wild nights, and we're so wide awake
And if just for once
You would just shut your mouth
And listen for a change

# Hudson House

When the other members of my first band and I rehearsed, we would all congregate in a disused building on the outskirts of Great Yarmouth.

It was risky business, having to climb a rotten, narrow wooden staircase with copious amounts of instruments and electrical equipment. The room itself was located on the first floor of the old warehouse, and to the side were several wooden doors, which opened outward, creating quite a risk to anyone who may step too close to them. I can only assume they were used in order for deliveries to be made from cranes, lifting supplies to the first floor.

As I looked out upon the buildings opposite, I became acutely aware of the faded name which was painted upon the long, grey, faded wall: Hudson House. The name struck me as a title which would suit a song, so I quickly set about writing some lyrics, keen to ensure my fellow bandmates did not beat me to it.

The song which followed told the story of a fictional character who lived within Hudson House. He was a loner, with no friends or family. He had little communication with the outside world, with his only joy coming from the sounds of the band which drifted though the air.

Down at Hudson House there is a man
And he sits alone at night
But, no, he knows no plans
Yet, he's doing alright

For him, the days and the nights, they drag him down
And he's living life alone
The only sense he sees
Are the sounds of the bands he knows

Every time he runs, he learns to see
That it's not just a state of mind
He is only there, you see
Just to tell you "yours is mine"

It's hard to see he's got a state of mind
Living his life along the white line
His mind sits wrong, so he's going back
Back to where he belongs
'Cause I know he's living wrong

As he sleeps, the morning sun will scream
And it wakes him up to life
Surely now this means

That he's doing something right?

It's hard to see he's got a state of mind
Living his life along the white line
His mind sits wrong, so he's going back
Back to where he belongs
'Cause I know he's living wrong

# Now I See

You make me see  all I should see
That's why my only belief  is you and me

On the days where I'm so fucking down
You'll pick me up when you come on back round

Now I see
I know it's hard
So don't give up on me
Now I see
I need you forever
So, darling, let us be

You make me feel all I should feel
In my times of need I'm unsure what's real

You come on back and smile at me
The love I need is a hunger that you feed

Now I see
For all my days
You are the one I need
Now I see
You're the only one
Who makes me believe

You make me know all I should know
That I'm worthwhile, you know I'll never go

The past was hard, but now we move
Forward now I love everything you do

Now I see
You're the only one
That I'll ever need
Now I see
Tomorrow never knows
So, let it be

# Something That We Used to Be

I have been listening to the Beatles since 2000, when the *1* album was released - a collection of the group's number one hits from 1962 to 1970. Naturally, my discovery of the Beatles led to me listening to John, Paul, George, and Ringo's solo works.

John Lennon's particular style profoundly affected me in the way I feel about music. I connected to his songs in such a way that I had never associated with any art form previously. I related to his words and the stories behind the music, feeling as though some songs were written about my own experiences and feelings. Lennon's style of writing was often autobiographical - he used his art to express his emotions - good or bad. I adopted this style of writing very early on - I respected Lennon for it and I soon learnt that it allowed me to express myself - by writing from the heart.

One example of my adoption of this process is 'Something (That We Used To Be)', which I composed in 2015.

I took heed of Lennon's style and methodology, which led to an increase in my volume of writing. This is one of my personal favourites amongst my collection, created when I felt unsure which way was up.

We were blue when the skies were grey
We were summer when the winter came
We were up when we both fell down
It was something that we used to be

We were two when we felt as one
We were warmth when the cold had gone
We were smiling when the world just cried
It was something that we used to be

So, whilst I sit around and I try to forget
All the things that we used to say
Basking in my own self-pity
When I know it will be okay
I close my eyes and all I see
Is a world and it doesn't need me
When you're left with nothing
And you don't come running
It was something that we used to be

We were love when all we knew was hate
We were open when they closed the gate
We were light when everything was dark

It was something that we used to be

We were hope when everything was lost
We were there when all the lines were crossed
We were pain when all the hurt went away
It was something that we used to be

# Plastic Entertainment

In 2001, a New Zealand-based television show, *Popstars*, changed the music industry and a proportion of televised entertainment, almost beyond recognition. Eventually being sold to over fifty countries, the talent show paved the way for countless similar shows, such as *Britain's Got Talent* and *The X Factor*.

Fast-forward over two decades and we are still drowning in television shows which are based on that same format, resulting in creating artists which draw in millions of pounds' worth of revenue.

Love it or loath it, it's here to stay, and shows no signs of letting up. As long as it sells, they will continue to make it.

In respect of musical creation, I am a traditionalist – my passion is for musicians, those who create their art from nothing more than a pen, a piece of paper, and perhaps an instrument. Many of the most popular and best-selling songs in history were composed by one or two people, simply using their passion to create art.

Nowadays, many artists have teams of writers around them, and the songs are manufactured in a way to attract as much revenue as possible. That's not to say that such songs are necessarily bad, but they are simply churned out only as a money-making process. It all feels so fake to me, so plastic...

You don't seem to have much to say
In a world that screams for more
You keep your feelings locked away
In a place that seems so secure

You speak the words that others feel
You're a shadow of the industry
You hide behind a wall of people
Your friends feel that you're lucky

It's all plastic entertainment
And the whole world's an open door
It's all plastic entertainment
And we don't want to hear it any more

So, the times they come when you're alone
Only to swallow your pain and run
Well, come on back as a different person
Now you've faded like the sun

And it's all plastic entertainment

I'm knocking my head against a wall
It's all plastic entertainment
And we don't want to listen any more

# This Town

During the time in which I wrote 'This Town', nightlife across the United Kingdom was in full swing. Pubs and clubs were plentiful and people would think nothing of going out of an evening and getting drunk beyond all comprehension, and spending most of their weekly wages for the pleasure.

Being a young man, I succumbed to the magnetism of local nightlife, albeit I gravitated towards the venues which hosted live musicians. Regardless, it would be a frequent sight to see grown adults acting like juveniles, whilst shouting inaudible mumblings whilst trying to crack one another's skulls open.

As with countless other towns, my home town appeared scenic, calm, and inviting during those warm, summer days. Once the sun set, things seemed to change.

Life in this town is easily misleading
I get around, but I've still got this feeling
Are you coming down, or are you high as the ceiling?
Look what you've found – a life unappealing to me

I look on every corner as people stand around
Dealing with their issues, the only way they know how
It's not a simple case of misconception
When this town crumbles down in a cloud of depression

Make a plan, take my hand, and do what you can
Just don't give it up, it's so rough in this town
Just turn right around as the walls crumble down
In a derelict border, there's nothing here, man, for me

You stand and you stare with your attitude
Like it's such a hard job, just not to be rude
It's not a simple case of misunderstanding
Take one look at me and already I'm branded as a no one

I can't handle life in this town
The people and the places are what's bringing me down
I must make a move and get out right now
Because I can't handle life in this town, no more

# (Sweet) Marie

One of the most prevalent themes in song and poetry is undoubtedly that of love. The theme is found in the earliest of writings, and will forever be a basis of every form of art. It is therefore unsurprising that I have frequently written about love.

We, as people, often find it very easy to criticise, to pick holes in something, and to talk ill of others. What we often find difficult is to praise, to encourage, and to tell others the many ways in which they are beautiful. I am as guilty of this as the next person and there have been many times when I have written down or had positive thoughts about another, but have failed to express that in an overt manner.

'(Sweet) Marie' was written in March 2017, as a tribute to my daughter's mum, and to this day remains one of my favourite pieces I have written, and always proves popular when I perform it as a song in public.

She will heal all the deepest scars
She will brighten the fading stars
Because she is (sweet) Marie

She will fill all the deepest holes
She'll hold so tight and never let go
Because she is (sweet) Marie

When you're under the weather
You just cannot be found
You're counting your days
And you bury your head in the ground
But she will be Marie

She will always be right there
Show you love and show she cares
Because she will be Marie

When you're under the weather
You just cannot be found
You're counting your days
And you bury your head in the ground
But she will be Marie
(Sweet) Marie

# Back Seat

I take a back seat to your life
I see the side you decided to hide
I know the only place that you will ever be
Is standing by my side
I see the underworld in a cold storm
It's like a clearing of my mind
I know this path that I will choose to follow
Will lead to the end of a life
These things are wrapped around my gaze
And it seems that I can't escape
They build me up and chase me down
Into a face that just can't amaze
But everybody's divine
We all have to walk a line
It seems so hard to find (to me)

# Me and the Messiah

Besides love, faith must surely be one of the most notable subjects within literature.

I have questioned my faith since I was twelve years old, when I had a near-fatal accident, and almost drown. I vividly recall the day I believed I was going to die. Whilst being violently thrown around by the grasp of the sea's currents, I looked up at the sky above, and begged; 'Please God, help me'. As the overpowering torrents pulled me beneath the waves, something seemingly took hold of me. As I emerged above the surface, I found myself within reaching distance of the river's edge – close enough to take hold and prevent my impending doom.

As much as I believe someone – or something – was looking out for me that day, I have always challenged my own beliefs and questioned what may be out there beyond our realms of understanding or perception. I wrote 'Me and the Messiah' as an outlet for the questions I often asked and the challenges that faith brought upon me.

I know what He's trying to do
He's trying to break me down
No matter the path that I choose
He'll flip it upside down

I'm always the last one to know
That failure's my only success
Why don't my roots ever grow
When I'm faced with the next of His tests?

I'll chase it and race it
Replace it and face it alone
I'm disgraced and misplaced
I can't show my face any more

I stand in the corner alone
Praying that someone will know
That I don't want to live life alone
What I grab, it always just goes

I'll see it, I'll feel it
Believe it, I want him to know
I'm fighting and writing
I can't seem to give up anymore

# American Dream

When I was twelve, my mum and her partner, 'Bob', took me to Orlando, Florida. I found America exhilarating. Everything seemed so extravagant and exciting. Ever since, I have always wanted to explore the rest of America and have been lucky enough to take a brief trip to New York City, which is a truly remarkable place to behold.

Through the medium of television, movies, and influential musicians such as Bruce Springsteen and Johnny Cash, we are sold what we feel is the 'American dream', but is it really so blissful?

The history of the United States is incredibly captivating, but a fractured one as well. Regardless, it is an incredible country that holds the potential of being all that someone may dream it to be.

'American Dream' is a fictional story of adventures across a foreign land, enjoying all of which it has to offer and to explore.

It's etched in South Dakota
Through the islands of New York
The strips of sweet Nevada
And the Carolina war

I've been lost in Central Park
Struck by the Liberty Bell
Watched the Texas revolution
Dived a Yellowstone well

We ride on through to Cali'
Right on down Sixty-Six
Breathe the air of Miami
Find St. Louis, get my kicks

I've been drunk in New Orleans
Crossed the Golden Gate Bridge
Signed all kinds of declarations
Jumped off Rushmore Ridge

We swam the falls of Niagara
Ran the roads throughout D.C.
Climbed the Hollywood sign
Blessed where the towers used to be

I've jumped away from the canyon
Sat upon the grassy knoll

Signed the Book of Independence
And all before I grew too old

I can see the light that shines on me
Don't you want to be a part of
The American dream?

I can see the light that shines on me
Don't you want to be a part of
The land of the free?

# Life's a Weight

Am I alone for today
Or am I just dreaming
Of a world far away?
For tomorrow may come
And tomorrow I'll hear what you say

I hear whispers in the air
But just as they say
I can't hear what they bear
You speak down to me
So, I'll turn, and you'll know
That I just don't care

I don't waste no time
Seeing things I don't want to see
When they involve me
(They always involve me)
It's a time when it seems
For the wicked, there is no rest

All I can think is
You must just speak under your breath

Life's a weight that I've found
A weight on my shoulders
That I just can't pass around

I may seem like the kind of guy
Who waits and smiles
Hangs around for a while
Stands at the door looking lonely
Whilst trying to find the key

The only want for success
Is the price that you pay
There's a price that you miss
Don't challenge the weight of the world
She's ready to hit

So, yes, life's a weight that I've found
A weight on my shoulders
That I just can't pass around

# Long Road Home

A message of love can come in many forms and contexts, not least the love you show for someone you have lost. We all lose people throughout our lives and death is, undoubtedly, one of the most difficult things we have to face up to.

A short time after '(Sweet) Marie' was written, my step-father, Robert 'Bob' Charles Dyble, passed away a matter of months after being diagnosed with lung cancer. He was just 63 years of age.

Despite previously experiencing loss in my family, Bob's passing was particularly difficult to come to terms with as nobody expected it to happen. Nobody should die at 63.

Cancer kills over 80,000 people a year in the UK alone, but none of us expect it to happen. It is one of those subjects we shy away from, rather than face up to. When my time came to face up to it, I addressed my feelings by writing 'Long Road Home'.

A personal touch in this song is the last line, 'just be sure to be homeward bound'. Bob was an avid fan of 50s and 60s music, including that of Simon and Garfunkel.

When you keep on trying, but you feel like crying
And nothing seems to go your way
So, the problems keep coming, you feel like running
And you never know quite what to say

It's a long road home
But sometimes you've got to go slow
Yes, it's a long road home
You may never know which way to go

If you feel all alone, the time goes slow
You never know which way is up
When you feel you've got to go
All the answers should be 'no'
Then you realise enough is enough

It's a long road home
But sometimes you've got to go slow
Yes, it's a long road home
You may never know which way to go

Because it's the heart aches that bring you down
But it's love that must be found
When the heart break comes around
Just be sure to be homeward bound

# Big Bad World

I thought you wanted it all
Play up until your final curtain call?
But everybody sees
The lies that you do talk
And all the deceit in your eyes

Are your lines crossed again?
Confusing times when
You're your own best friend
What are you going to do next?
Don't run too fast
You might not think like the rest

I don't wish you any harm at all
I just hope that you find what you're looking for
It's a big, bad world
I don't think you're ready at all

What are you trying to do?

What you don't have
You steal 'cause you want it too
It's like I read your mind
I'm just afraid of what it is I may find

I see a shadow on my back
If I sang a line
Then you'll sing it right back
People come, and people go
But you can only learn
From what you don't already know

I don't wish you any harm at all
I just hope that you find what you're looking for
It's a big, bad world
I don't think you're ready at all

# The Busker's Blues

As I began to perform in front of family, friends, and strangers, my confidence to allow others to hear my voice gradually grew, but it took many years before I felt confident enough to perform any of my own songs with the passion I felt at the time in which I wrote them. I remember many occasions that the blood would instantaneously rush to my head and I would sweat, shake, and ultimately crumble under the pressure. I suffered from stage fright to the point where I would often make excuses to not perform at all, just to save myself the immense amount of anxiety I would suffer.

To help with my self-confidence, I would busk in my local towns and cities, sometimes alone, but more often than not, with other musical friends. We never did it for the money, just the experience.

There are some incredible performers who busk for leisure, or to earn a living, and it takes real guts to stand in the middle of a street and perform your art – in whichever form that may be.

'The Busker's Blues' was my attempt at trying to understand how some of them may have felt.

I think I've been sitting here
For way too long
I've been trying to find my way back home
For so long
Because it's a long, long way back home
For someone

I'm standing at the station
In need of education
I'm needing someone by my side
Because the nights are so wild
I just left my job, I couldn't stand it
I'm fine!

I'm waiting on the underground
Singing songs for lonely crowds
Making the money I need
Time's passing by, so I'm needing more time
I'm looking to search out the speed
Walking away, someone tells me to stay on my knees

I'm running away from the people who say
'Come along and play us a song'
They don't know my needs, as I lay upon the streets
And it seems that they've got it all wrong

But I'm not fussed now
Because it seems I've been doing this for so long

# Changing Lives

As we grow older, and hopefully wiser, our perspectives change and we look upon the world from a different point of view.

Once we leave school, we tend to lose many of our childhood friends because, quite simply, life takes over. We go on to new things; we fall in love; we go to work; we have children. But some people choose a different path, a darker way to live. It is likely that we can all think of at least one person this reminds us of. 'Changing Lives' was written about one such person.

Where do all the good times seem to go
When you're all alone just getting stoned?
How many times must you walk that lonely road
And still not know where to go?

You're going down in your mind and losing your soul

To a place that only you know
Your sun has risen for the very last time
And everywhere are happy souls

What you see with your eyes is no surprise to me
A world of mindless thoughts
The person who was there a long, long time ago
Has gone, but you still want more

You creep along a long and winding corridor
To face yet another door
Everything that was once held in your hands
Has now just fell to the floor

We live in an age of self-demise
Everywhere there's changing lives
Everyone is full of shit
I don't know why everyone's changing lives

Everything that you thought you once knew
Has all blown away with the wind
Reminiscing images reminding
Self-confessions of every sin

The times are changing, now what's amazing
In a world where you never win
Is that you can't screw up only nearly enough
And throw it all away in the bin

We live in an age of self-demise

Everywhere there's changing lives
Everyone is full of shit
I don't know why everyone's changing lives

Only now are you really starting to realise
What you nearly became
The truth becomes clearer every day
Because you know you're not the same

But it's never your fault, you just turn your head
There's always someone else to blame
The person that was there before has disappeared
I don't even know your name

# The Reasons Why

What's been has gone, now all that's over
We've been so strong for one another
No more hard times, a smooth road ahead
No more harsh lies, forget what we both said

I look up front, as I open my eyes
Within my life I'm feeling paralysed
Yes, I know things just can't get any worse
But I know we'll get what we deserve

Whilst everything is left behind
A silent time's a way to cry
And in your heart, there you will find
The answers and the reasons why

# Equanimity

Sometimes songs and poems just happen with little thought or planning, as was the case with this particular piece.

Written in one brief session, the poem was created simply due to me hearing the word 'equanimity' the first time. I found the word to be rather thought-provoking and so, I wished to utilise it in verse.

The definition of equanimity is 'calmness and composure, especially in a difficult situation'. With this in mind, it makes the words of this poem somewhat more understandable and relatable.

It tells a fictional story of someone who is used for sexual gratification, and their sense of self-worth is diminishing, because of their unpleasant experiences.

You say you've got problems
You're not 'getting enough'

Because you thought you had it
But you're just out of the rough
I know it isn't easy
When you're living a lie
When the person you love
Becomes all you despise

When you nights and your days
All just roll into one
You hide your wasted mind
In a shadow of 'fun'
All of the issues
Are what's bringing you down
You're facing wrong directions
Never homeward bound

You've got to:
Stop.
Breathe.
Wait there and see.
That nothing in this life comes easily.
You've got to:
Wait.
Look.
Stand tall and be
Everything you ever wanted to be.

Drawn to emotions
That you just can't stand
With no one to guide you

With their helping hand
You write down your number
In an old phone box
When you're hoping you're the one
That has all the 'good luck'

I know how you feel
When you tell me you're down
I've been there before
When I was younger than now
All the world's weight
Seems to fall upon you
You lay there in the evenings, thinking
*What do I do?*

You've got to:
Stop.
Breathe.
Wait there and see.
That nothing in this life comes easily.
You've got to:
Wait.
Look.
Stand tall and be
Everything you ever wanted to be
Equanimity

# Every Time

Sometimes my technique for writing may mean that there are significant gaps between starting a project and finishing it. Frequently I have part-wrote a piece, only to return to it days, weeks, or even years later.

One particular song I wrote, 'Every Time', was written in two parts, with several months between the first and the latter halves. The first section was written during a relationship, the second half post-relationship. You may notice the shift in tone.

Every time she smiles, she smiles for me
Every time she breathes, it's a sigh of relief
Every time she walks, it's a milestone
Every time she's there I'm never alone, no, no

She sees me when I sleep
She knows when I'm awake

Nothing in this life
Can simply be 'give or take'

She feeds me when I'm hungry
She mends me back to health
She'll knock me off my feet
For just being myself

Now these days have started
Don't you leave me broken hearted, walk away
She left me home and lonely
It's just like she doesn't know me today

Every time she lies, she lies for me
Every time she speaks, it is full of deceit
Every time she writes, she's putting me down
Every time she sings, I'm never around, no, no

Once I was a poor boy
She made my life so rich
It wouldn't be so bad
If she was not such a bitch

She makes me smile and laugh
Then scares me half to death
She stops my heart from beating
So, I cannot catch a breath

Yes, she left me home and lonely
So she never has to see me again

She was my one and only
Now she only drives me round the bend

Every time she smiles
Every time she breathes
Every time she lies
Every time she leaves

# Diary

Many years ago, I formed a relationship with a female, who I considered a friend. As time passed, I come to realise that she saw me as more than that.

One evening, she allowed me to read her diary as she wanted me to see how she felt, and what difficulties she was going through at that moment in time. I wrote 'Diary' as a response to what I read within those pages.

You let everybody read about your life
You don't hold back because that's just not right
You fill the page with imagination
You tell tales about infatuations with me

It seems you're not afraid to speak your mind
In a world that decides
You're good enough for one night
Because you've got the strength to say you feel nothing

To you it's just nothing
But nothing means something to me

It all just seems that there's more to the story behind
Closed doors conceal what I feel I am needing to find
And it winds me up
Just to think I'm not hearing the truth
Like it's all screwed up
Thrown away like yesterday's news

You're not ashamed when you're crossing the line
You're getting old, but your mind is not wise
Alone in the world, feel the suffocation
The hands round your throat tell you
Your life's amazing to lead

You're weeping alone because you feel so abandoned
Fool on the hill, now you're cold and you're stranded
Your mind has no place, you can't feel it no more
In your life it rains, I know, but in mine it just pours

It all just seems that there's more to the story behind
Closed doors conceal what I feel I am needing to find
And it winds me up
Just to think I'm not hearing the truth
Like it's all screwed up
Thrown away like yesterday's news

The words in your verses, they relentlessly hurt us
Put a strain on emotions, does this life deserve us?

Touch what you feel. Can you feel suffocation?
It stemmed from the love and your infatuation with me

# Valley Virtue

The Oxford English Dictionary's definition of the word 'virtue' is 'behaviour showing high moral standard', and it is this of which I based the words of 'Valley Virtue' upon.

Time has not allowed me to recall who I wrote the poem about, I do, however, recollect it being inspired by how the subject would always put themself down, or doubted their own abilities. Regardless of such attributes, it was clear to me that they were a good person and their moral compass was firmly pointing in the right direction.

I took the personal attribute of a 'virtue' and transformed it into a place, in this case, a valley. By doing so, it allowed me to imagine that such qualities are a destination of which we strive to reach.

Endeavouring to be someone who behaves in a manner of which shows a high moral standard is an attribute we should all strive for.

The sun is high in the sky
Of the Valley Virtue
The high treetops and the rocks
With an ocean so blue
You see, it is not so bad being you
No, it is not so bad being you

The love and the push and the shove
That you need to get through
The days as you play the same games
Because you need a break too
You see, it's not so bad being you
No, it is not so bad being you

The birds they will sing
Let them ring as they sing it to me
The air that I breathe drops beneath
I believe I can see
You see, it's not so bad being you
No, it is not so bad being you

The paths that may cross
Through the deepest of troughs you may walk
With your heart on your sleeve as you strive to relieve
Everything that came before
You see, it's not so bad being you
No, it is not so bad being you

So, let's bring it together, let us sing
We can just remember all the things
Behind the reasons we share the things we do
I hope you see me, because I do sure see you
You see, it's not so bad just being two
It's not so bad being two, just me and you

# Slipping Away

Completed in October 2011, 'Slipping Away' began life as a story, talking of a fictional third person, who was facing tough times. I wished to convey how I pushed them to carry on, despite the difficulties they were wading through.

The more I delved into developing the content, the more I came to realise that it was not a fictional story, but indeed a very autobiographical collection of feelings. Inspired by personal events of the time, I was telling myself what I should do, during a time in which my mental health was declining, and I needed some direction. By the concluding verse, I was telling myself not to give up. Turning things around, I was no longer slipping away.

As one door closed, another one opened
I can see through the other side
It may be a tight squeeze. Open up the door please

I'm ripping up a pack of lies

I have a hole in my jeans, and it's tearing at the seams
I haven't got a penny to my name
I'm pushing up the road, as I carry heavy loads
I'm living in the shadow of dreams

You've got to push hard, boy
You've got to carry on
You've got to find your feet now
Before it's all gone

And I feel like I'm slipping away now
I have not got nobody to blame
The feelings inside, I just can't hide
Because I feel like I'm slipping away

The pennies on my eye and I'm all out of luck
It's all going wrong, I can see
Got to think happy thoughts
Thank the stars and thank the Lord
That I've really got what I need

For a moment there, well, I thought it was gone
It seems that it's all working out
Got to walk feet first, even though the hazards hurt
I'm not living in doubt

You've got to work hard, boy
You have to carry on

You have to settle down now
Before it's all gone

I'm no longer slipping away now
I never had nobody to blame
The feelings inside, I just can't hide
I'm no longer slipping away

# If You Ever

## (For Her)

If you ever need some time, girl
Don't be afraid
To take a little 'you time'
Take it any day
If you ever need somebody
I won't be far
If you ever need a shoulder
Or a caring heart
I will be there, by your side
If you ever need some love, girl
You can have mine

If you ever need to daydream
Come sleep by my side
Rest your weary little head, now
Let it rest upon mine
If you ever need to sleep here

Then close your eyes
You can dream a little dream, now
Get lost in your mind
I will be here, by your side
If you ever need some love, girl
You can have mine

# I'm Just Like You

Inspired by the works of Bob Dylan, 'I'm Just Like You' was my first attempt at writing what I considered being a piece with more depth, written when I was about 20.

The inspiration came in the form of a realisation that someone close to me had a particular personality trait of which I did not like. Accepting that I had that very same trait, I set about ensuring that I did not become just like them.

It's easy to judge by what you see
But you don't know just by looking at me
You decide by what you've found
I'll get my feet right back upon the ground

Everybody knows the score
I don't know no one who hasn't been here before
Whilst you frown upon all who isn't you

It takes a wise man to overcome a fool

I'm just like you
I don't want to be just like you

Whilst he's feeling that he's right
He turns around and now he's struck upon his life
What hides inside his mind is always wrong
He lies awake and wonders, 'til the morning comes

I'm just like you
I don't want to be just like you
Yes, I'm just like you
But I don't want to be just like you

# India

So many years, they all pass us by
Let's cut to the chase, you're walking on fine wire
India, oh, India, you're on fire

You've got another secret that you need to confess
Underneath the pressure, you always do your best
India, oh, India, you are blessed

You've always been so strong
You're never, ever wrong
You've always been alright
When you're taken for a ride
You won't forget the lights
At the end of the night
You'll always be the one
Who I'll never see denied

Never been one for always taking your time
Got to jump right in, take a leap on the line

India, oh, India, you'll be fine

You've always been so straight
With every road that you will take
You've always been alone
In your heart and in your soul
You'll never, ever call
You'll catch yourself when you may fall
It's only ever you
Standing tall against life's walls

# Lonely Cause

Approximately 280 million people worldwide suffer from depression. 19% of adults have been diagnosed with depression. 109 million working days are lost every year within the UK because of depression-related absence.

With such troubling statistics, why is it that so many of us are still afraid to talk about our mental health? I was one of them, but I soon learnt that depression cannot be managed effectively by yourself.

'Lonely Cause', and the next composition, 'Midlife Crisis at 22', were written during a stage in my life when I was struggling with my own mental health. They acted as an outlet to something I knew I needed assistance with, but was unsure how to get such help.

Sitting around, never doing much
Whilst everything is never enough for me
Staring at the walls, I'm a lonely cause

Like living in the shadows won't ever set me free

I know that I say this every day
But a part of me thinks that I will never die
Because I know that I won't live forever
A part of me that's not so clever will try

Don't believe in me
I will only let you down
Don't wish me free
I deserve what I've got now

Walking down a road that I've never known
The others in the world don't ever seem to see
That it seems some days that there's an easier way
I find it all a struggle, so I'll just let it be

Just believe in me
I will never let you down
I dream I'm free
I deserve what I've got now

# Midlife Crisis at 22

I feel like I've been picked up and thrown down
Because this life's a mess
Like I've fallen away from my mind now
I've got a taste for creation
It's a way just to say how I feel
But there's too much to say
On the days where I'm just watching the wheels

It's like a mid-life crisis at 22
Sitting on my arse, not knowing what to do
It's a tough life to lead when you don't know what to do
When the melodies you sing just come out like the blues

I can feel all the strain of the things
I can't take any more
It seems I'm dragging me down
Now I'm out cold on the floor
I don't know where I've been
I don't know where I'm heading today
Won't you please take my hand?

Guide me somewhere far, far away

It's like a mid-life crisis at 22
Sitting on my arse, not knowing what to do
It's a tough life to lead when you don't know what to do
When the melodies you sing just come out like the blues

So, it seems that my head hurts
More than once today
I've got a taste for this life
But it all seems such a strain
When everything brings you down
You just can't fight back
Just rely on yourself
Because nobody else has your back

It's like a mid-life crisis at 22
Sitting on my arse, not knowing what to do
It's a tough life to lead when you don't know what to do
When the melodies you sing just come out like the blues

# The Man

On March 8, 2016, it was announced that Sir George Martin, one of the most successful and influential music producers in history, had passed away, aged 90.

Martin lived an incredible life, and will always be remembered as the man who said 'yes' to the Beatles. He was always considered a kind, gentle soul, and was respected all over the world for his work within the music industry.

'The Man' was written on the day of Sir George's passing, and is my telling of when he and John, Paul, George and Ringo first worked with one another.

Met up in an old beaten room with a light on
Set up the band and the man asked the boys
'What's your best song?'
Melodies played in the air and the man said
'It's okay,
It's not your best, but you won't regret coming my way'

He said...

'Sing me a song, take the whole world on, let 'em see
I can't be wrong, this is where you belong, with me
Show 'em what you've got, take it to the top, and away
This is your life, your choice, your whole decade'

So it begins, hear the songs, let 'em ring in your ears
The boys, they will sing for so long
They'll reduce you to tears
On the lanes, in the planes
Down the Abbey, oh darling, get back, my dear
Going insane to sustain all the happiness, all these years
He said...

'Sing me a song, take the whole world on, let 'em see
I can't be wrong, this is where you belong, with me
Show 'em what you've got, take it to the top, and away
This is your life, your choice, your whole decade'

# Pass Me By

Once I completed high school, I went straight into full-time employment. Unsure which direction I wanted my life to take, I jumped between numerous professions, finding little satisfaction in the work I was doing.

One area I worked in was retail. It was during a particularly arduous shift that I wrote 'Pass Me By', on the back of a paper receipt.

During my time within that particular job, I quickly learnt how thoroughly unpleasant some people can be towards those who are there to help. A minority of customers would show little regard for manners, often failing to simply say 'please' and 'thank you'.

I quickly found myself hoping that those within the minority would not approach me, but simply pass me by.

I sit there by the window, watching millions pass me by
I ask the same old questions

The answers are still a lie
Pass me by

Everywhere I look, I see, mindless thoughts behind the eyes
They're more confused again today
More strung up than you or I
Pass me by
Pass me by

I stand there by the door and I struggle to realise why
I put up with all the shit I hate
And the people who I despise
Pass me by

Everyone I meet they need something, God knows why?
I know that they will never say
They're more stuck up than you and I
Pass me by
Pass me by

# Reminisce

So long friends, goodbye for now
I feel like we have lost touch somehow
It feels like a lifetime since I've seen you
I wish I could share all the things I've been through

I often think of all the things I miss
Drinking games and singing songs like this
I can't forget the things we used to do
When all I really want to do is be with you

I spend days watching time roll away
Sitting on my doorstep, whilst my mind changed
I reminisce of laughter, smiles and pain
As I walk home in the morning, in the pouring rain

# What He Needs to Say

Out on the street, when the night is blind
Going to give a little light, going to see what he'll find
No, it doesn't come easy, no, it doesn't come hard
It won't come in the daytime, and the night's a little dark
He can give a little something, a little piece of his heart
To jump out of his comfort, is a jump too far
He can give it all almighty. he can put up a fight
He can steal your religion, be your Jesus Christ

He'll say he is 'like an angel'
I say he is like a war
He'll say he is 'one in a million'
I'll say he is one to deplore

It might seem strange, from an outside view
To seek a little something, when that something is you
But don't hold your breath, when he's saying out loud
'Please come with me, I will take you out'
Don't you fall for that beauty and charm

He speaks the right words, but intends the wrong
He'll slip you a line, take you on your way
This way is how he likes it, his way is your last day

He'll say he is 'like an angel'
I say he is like a war
He'll say he is 'one in a million'
I'll say he is one to deplore

# Secret Times

Whilst out with friends one evening, we were in one of the local clubs when, far across the room, a female caught my eye. She was beautiful, and it appeared as though I, too, captured her eye attention also. As though it was a scene from a movie, she seemingly vanished, as dozens of other people walked amongst us, never to be seen by me again.

For what was such a brief and meaningless encounter, it seemed to stick in my mind for such a long time. Twenty years later, I wonder if she will read this and wonder, *is it about me?*

I don't know who you are
I have yet to know your name
I saw you standing there
I could see that you weren't afraid
Will I ever see you again?

Under the minor lights
Under the signs and secret times
Something is waking up
Something is creeping up inside
I hope that I see you again

I have lost your face
I have lost control this time
Picking up the thoughts
Wishing that you weren't away
Searching everywhere
Hoping just to find you there
Somewhere soon

# Stay With Me

I'm asking you once, I hope you'll say
You'll stay with me
I can't be alone, I'm too afraid
Of what I'll see

Go capture my thoughts, and cling to my dreams
I'm walking bare
My mind's in unrest, not a happy place
In case you care

No one knows what it's like
When you're alone, like me
No one knows what it's like
To be scared

Go sing me a song, a happy song
That'll make me smile
Go dream a dream of a melody
But take your time

No one knows what it's like
When you're alone, like me,
No one knows what it's like
To be me

# Troubled Boy

Have you seen the boy who got the troubles?
It's such a shame that he burst his own bubble
He waits in line to waste away
Tracks his mis-steps between now and his next payday

He must admit that he lost his way
'Cause our troubled little boy has seen better days
What, with the love and the lust and the life that he's lost
Our troubled little boy has been double-crossed
And it's so sad to see him go

He started off in lands of woes and wonders
Until his world came crashing down like thunder
He lost his name and face in all the places, like the dust
The thing with our boy is he always has the words
But he never gained the trust

He'll soon admit that he lost his way
'Cause our troubled little boy has seen better days

What, with the love and the lust and the life that he's lost
Our troubled little boy has been double-crossed
And it's so sad to see him go

# Wait Another Day

Wait another day for the things you want to say
Take your time
There's such a bigger picture than you ever dreamed
In your mind
All will be fine
Take a step back for a minute
Watch your mind
Hold your thoughts inside, your heart will swim the tide
To come undone
There's more to this damn life than you ever dreamed
So, feel as one
You are divine
I'll take another step and look at you
For some time
All will be fine

# Went Outside

I turned off my mind, went outside for a while
Then it seemed like I felt like new
I cleared out my thoughts as I opened the doors
That lead to a homegrown truth

It's alright when you sit inside your mind
But to leave it behind, you can never define
The distance between love and the life that you find

I opened my eyes to the world outside
And it seemed like I'd seen nothing
Whilst the future's so bleak and it hides what I seek
It's between here and 'something'

What goes around whilst you're playing the clown
Is what you'll miss, you'll never know
You walk alone on the emptiest roads
Now you feel like your life's a show

It's alright when you sit inside your mind
But to leave it behind, you can never define
The distance between love and the life that you find

# If You Ever

## (For Amelie)

As we come to the end of this volume of My Verses, it is only right that the last word is dedicated to my beautiful daughter, Amelie. She is my strength, my rock, my love.

Nothing can prepare you for parenthood. No amount of articles, videos, or guidance from others can ever allow you to contemplate the vast array of emotions you will continuously go through when you experience parenthood.

No matter how many times, your children make you want to tear your hair out the joy and love they provide trumps all the bad stuff one-hundred times over.

I always wanted to be a parent, and when Amelie came along, I was overjoyed. That joy extends to every single day, and will for the rest of my life. Amelie completes me.

Amelie, this is for you.

If you ever need love, you can have mine
If you ever must think, then please take your time
If you ever need a shoulder, come rest on me
If you ever have a vision, let me help you see
If you ever need hope, allow me to show
The love that I have, and allow it to grow
If you ever seek direction, I'll be your guide
If you ever need space, go run and hide
If you ever feel pain, allow me to care
If you ever need daddy, I will be there

# Final Thoughts

I would like to dedicate this book to everyone who has inspired its contents, because, without them, I would not have ever found the inspiration to write much of what I have included within this book.

Without one another, life would be a miserable, lonely place. Life is tough enough, without war, hate, pain, resentment, and suffering. What makes this life beautiful is the people within it. Support, guide, cherish and love one another, because life can be painfully short.

If you, yourself, have never tried your hand at writing, I wholeheartedly recommend it. Especially in difficult times. It is a form of expressionism and can act as a release for anything you may be feeling, whatever that may be.

If you have been affected by any of the subject matter within this book, you are *not* alone. Talk to someone if you are lonely. Don't be afraid to ask for help if you are depressed. If you are grieving, contact friends, family, or charities to help you. You are *not* alone.

If you have obtained this book for free, and if you are able, please donate to your chosen charity as a "thank you" to me. If you do not have a chosen charity, I politely request you to contribute to Cancer Research UK. They do an incredible job and may one day be the support you so need.

Thank you.
Adrian Young

❦ ⸱⸱❀⸱⸱ ❦

# Thank You

Thank you for taking the time to read *My Verses*. I hope it has been a pleasure for you to read.

As a special thank you, you can access exclusive content, discounts, and free gifts by signing up to my mailing list, which you can do by visiting:

https://www.adrianyoungauthor.com/mailing-list

You can also find me via  social media platforms:

Twitter: @A_Young_Author
Facebook: Adrian Young – Author

Please consider leaving a review for this book on Amazon and GoodReads. Thank you.

Printed in Great Britain
by Amazon